STEGOSAURUS

the DINOSAUR with the...

Spiky

Spine

H

Illus

Professor Michael J Benton – dinosaur consultant
Valerie Wilding – educational advisor
Ben Newth – researcher

Scholastic Children's Books,
Commonwealth House, 1-19 New Oxford Street,
London WC1A 1NU, UK

A division of Scholastic Ltd
London ~ New York ~ Toronto ~ Sydney ~ Auckland
Mexico City ~ New Delhi ~ Hong Kong

Published in the UK by Scholastic Ltd, 2003

Text copyright © Helen Greathead, 2003
Illustrations copyright © Mike Spoor, 2003

ISBN 0 439 97821 1

Contents

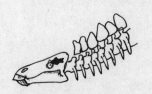

Contents

Introduction

If you're not sure how to say Stegosaurus,
just break the name into bits:

Steg-oh-sore-us

Say it slowly, then a bit faster.
Got it? Great! Now let's find
out what Stegosaurus was
really like.

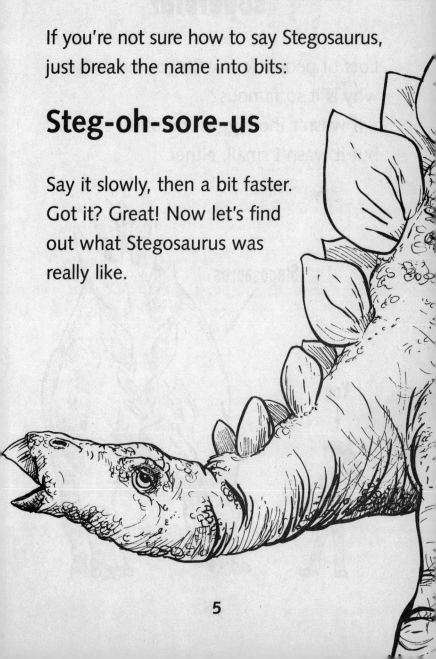

Stegosaurus is a bit of a superstar

Lots of people know Stegosaurus. But why is it so famous?

It wasn't the biggest dinosaur ever … but it wasn't small, either.

Stegosaurus

You

It wasn't the scariest dinosaur ever …
but it could fight if it had to.

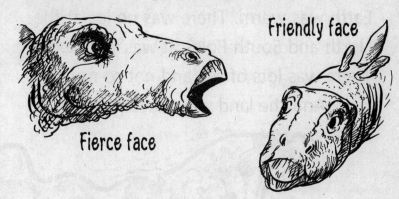

Friendly face

Fierce face

It wouldn't ever eat you … but it could
give you some nasty bruises!

A Stegosaurus
did it!

But Stegosaurus looked strange even
for a dinosaur! That's why people find
it so interesting.

And strange things were happening when Stegosaurus lived. The weather on Earth was warm. There was no ice at the North and South Poles. It was wet, too. There was lots of sea and not so much land. And the land was moving!

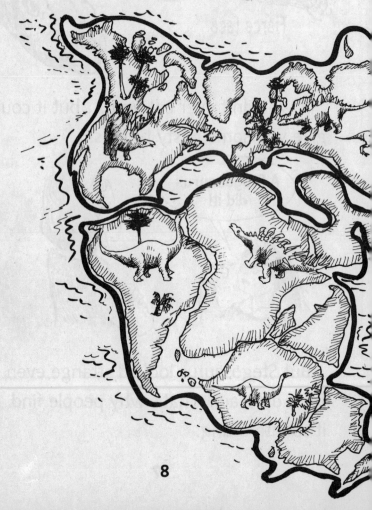

Once all the land was joined together. But when Stegosaurus was around the land started breaking into huge pieces. Very slowly these pieces became the continents we know today.

The land didn't have flowers ... or grass. But it did have loads of trees and plants ... and dinosaurs.

Giant Apatosaurus (ah-pat-oh-sore-us)
reached up to nibble the treetops. Little
Dryosaurus (dry-oh-sore-us) munched
on the plants underneath. And when the
dinosaurs slept, tiny, furry Dryolestes
(dry-oh-less-teez) crept out to feed –
without getting squashed!

A bird called Archaeopteryx (ark-ee-op-ter-ix) flew through the skies. It had teeth like a dinosaur and claws … on its wings!

Enormous crocodiles swam in the sea. They had flippers like fish!

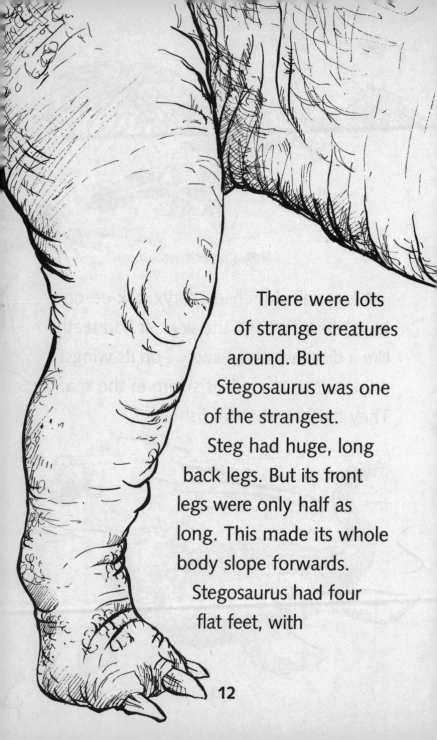

There were lots
of strange creatures
around. But
Stegosaurus was one
of the strangest.
Steg had huge, long
back legs. But its front
legs were only half as
long. This made its whole
body slope forwards.
Stegosaurus had four
flat feet, with

12

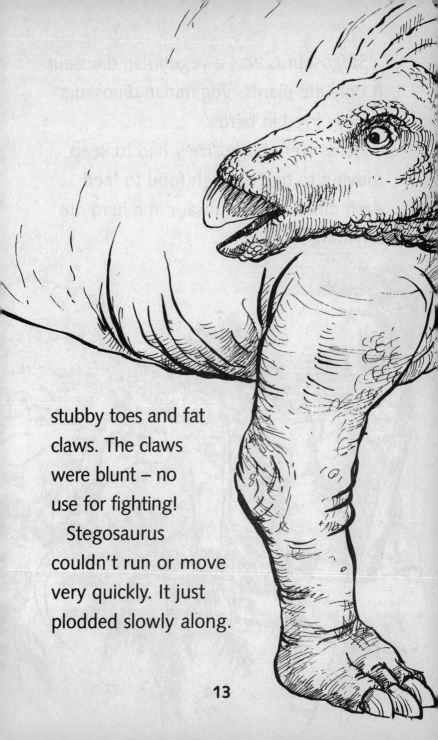

stubby toes and fat
claws. The claws
were blunt – no
use for fighting!
  Stegosaurus
couldn't run or move
very quickly. It just
plodded slowly along.

13

Stegosaurus was a vegetarian dinosaur. It only ate plants. Vegetarian dinosaurs usually lived in herds.

Herds were huge. They had to keep moving to find enough food to feed each dinosaur. A dinosaur in a herd ate anything it could.

But Stegosaurus liked to live alone.

Living alone meant that Steg could do what it liked.

Parp!

And *eat* what it liked. Living alone was good for Stegosaurus, because it was fussy about food!

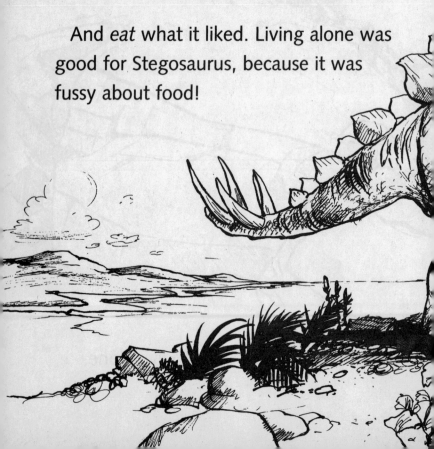

Steg didn't stretch up to the trees to find food, like other vegetarian dinosaurs. Its nose stayed near the ground to sniff out seeds and cones; sweet, green shoots and fat, juicy fruits.

This is a cycad (sigh-cad) plant.

Sharp, spiky leaves

Fat, juicy fruit

That fruit wasn't easy to get at. But
Steg wasn't easily put off.

Stegosaurus had
a hard, lumpy neck.
The sharp leaves
didn't scratch it.

Stegosaurus had
a funny little
head. The head
fitted neatly inside
the cycad plant.

Instead of front teeth it had
a horny beak. The beak
was just right for
nipping off the
fruit. Mmm,
tasty!

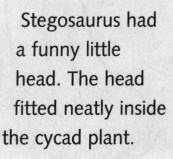

Behind the beak, Steg did have lots of teeth. But they didn't look anything like yours.

Stegosaurus tooth

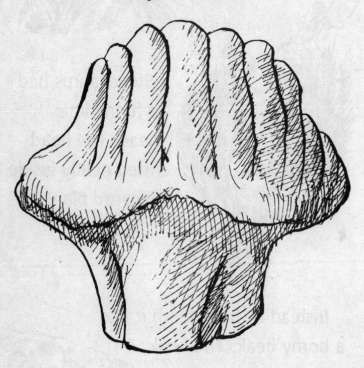

They were good for cutting leaves. They were good for mushing fruit. But Steg's teeth weren't very strong.

They were not good for chewing.

Gulp! Gulp!

So Stegosaurus swallowed food quickly.
And the food sloshed about in Steg's
tummy for days before coming out of the
other end!

Gurgle Phht!

Gulp

The strangest thing about Stegosaurus was its spiky back.

Scientists call the spikes "plates". The plates were made of bone and covered with skin.

The largest plate was this big

The smallest was this big

Scientists know why Steg's back legs were long and why its head was small, but after years and years of studying, they still don't know why it had spiky plates on its spine.

Stegosaurus and its spiky spine

Scientists like a good argument. And they've certainly argued a lot about Steg's plates. There are loads of ideas about what they were for.

Some say:

> The plates were used to attack other dinosaurs.

Hmmm, they do look sharp. But imagine having plates on your back. How would you use them to fight? It wouldn't be easy, would it?

Others say:

The plates helped Stegosaurus to protect itself.

Well, that makes sense, because the plates *looked* sharp and dangerous. In fact they were not sharp at all! But they made Stegosaurus seem bigger … and scarier than it really was.

A scientist, called Jim Farlow, had another idea. He studied fossils of the plates. Fossils are bones and traces of dinosaurs that have turned to rock over millions of years.

He noticed that the plates had grooves on each side.

Grooves   Grooves

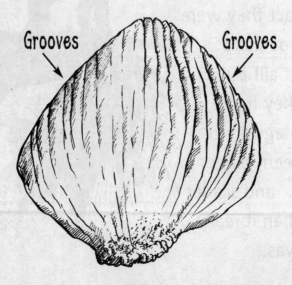

Maybe the grooves were for blood vessels? Blood vessels could carry blood from Steg's body through the plates.

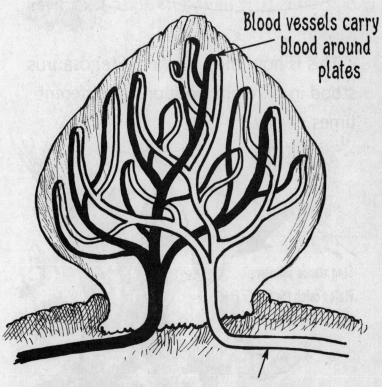

Blood vessels carry blood around plates

Blood flows through Steg's body

Now that sounds really strange, doesn't it? But it gave Jim Farlow an amazing idea...

Jim Farlow said:

The plates helped Stegosaurus to warm up and cool down!

This is how they worked. Stegosaurus stood in different positions at different times of day.

Morning:

Steg stands sideways. Plates catch the full heat of the sun

Blood warms up and flows round the body. Stegosaurus warms up

Afternoon:

Hot sun hits the edges of the plates. Blood in plates loses heat

Sides of plates keep out of the sun

Steg keeps cool in scorching sun!

Evening:

Cool wind blows through the plates. Blood cools down

Blood flows round the body. Stegosaurus cools down. It's ready to sleep

There was another reason why blood in Steg's plates might be really useful.

Stegosaurus lived in flat, open areas of land called plains. On the plains it could see a long way. It could spot danger a mile off. And danger could spot Stegosaurus.

Ceratosaurus (seh-rat-oh-sore-us) was a meat-eater. It had nasty, sharp teeth and claws. It was smaller than Stegosaurus. But stronger.

Here's what might have happened when the two dinosaurs met...

Ceratosaurus sees Stegosaurus. It notices the spiky plates. But it still thinks Stegosaurus looks tasty.

It gets a bit closer. Suddenly, the spiky plates flush fiery red. Wow, Stegosaurus looks fierce!

When Little Dryosaurus hops into the picture, Ceratosaurus chases after it. Forget Stegosaurus, Dryosaurus will be a much easier lunch!

So Stegosaurus was safe. Phew! Sending blood to its plates made Steg *look* really angry – and it didn't have to move a muscle!

But what happened when Steg really did get angry?

Stegosaurus gets very, very angry

Stegosaurus didn't usually do much more than plod around looking for food and eating.

But some things made it very, very angry.

• Another dinosaur trying to attack.

• Another Stegosaurus stealing its water! Water was as important as food to Stegosaurus. Without water any animal will die.

So Stegosaurus had to fight to survive.
But how?

It didn't have sharp teeth or claws.

Its spiky plates only *looked* sharp.

Well, one part of its body was
absolutely deadly …

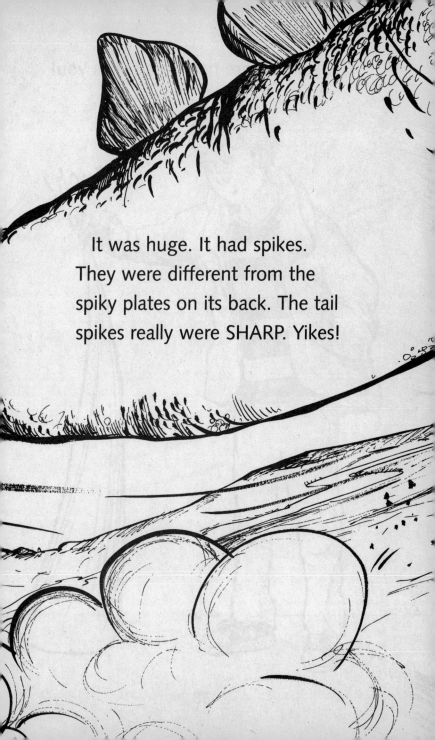

It was huge. It had spikes.
They were different from the
spiky plates on its back. The tail
spikes really were SHARP. Yikes!

The spikes were nearly as tall as you!

They were hard, but they weren't made of bone.

They were bone covered with horn, like the antlers on a deer.

Horn is a little bit bendy. It can make a really sharp point, too. So it's doubly deadly!

The tail was bendy, too. Lots of dinosaurs had stiff tails. But Steg's tail could really swish!

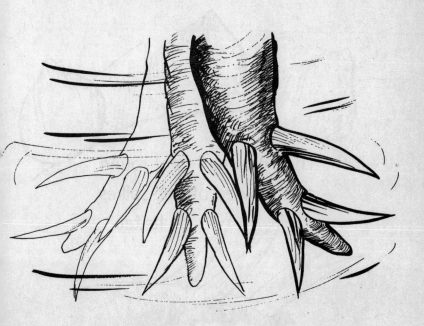

When Stegosaurus got angry, it quickly tucked in its head. There were no plates to protect its head. Steg showed off the plates on its neck instead.

Next Stegosaurus turned to the side – and showed off the plates on its spine.

Then it turned right round – and showed off the spikes on its tail.

Its short front
legs shuffled from
side to side.

It looked a bit
like Steg was
dancing!

Its strong back
legs helped to
swish the tail.

Then Stegosaurus attacked ...
backwards!

WHACK!
It knocked knees.

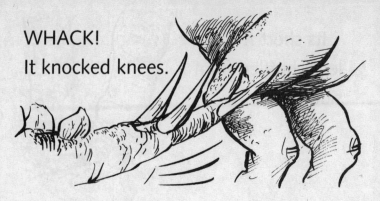

It bashed ankles.

It jabbed its tail spikes right into its attacker's body!

Stegosaurus didn't care where the tail swished. Wherever it hit was sure to cause damage.

Vegetarian dinosaurs had all sorts of weapons.

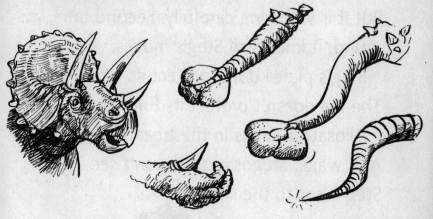

But Steg's tail was more deadly than all of them. One whack would send most dinosaurs running.

But Allosaurus was bigger than Stegosaurus and it was really mean. A hungry Allosaurus would come back and fight again.

Here's what might have happened:

Allosaurus is hurt after the first fight. But it is watching carefully. Second time round, it knows all Steg's moves.

Steg's plates don't protect its head. The tail doesn't protect its tummy.

Allosaurus hides in the trees. It waits. And waits. Stegosaurus doesn't see it. Steg turns to the side.

Allosaurus runs for Steg's tummy, jaws
wide open, claws ready.

Steg's tail doesn't get a chance to swish.

Allosaurus was a clever dinosaur.
Stegosaurus wasn't!

Stegosaurus isn't clever

Scientists can work out how clever a dinosaur was by looking at fossils of its skull. The soft, squishy bits of the body rot away when it dies. So you won't ever find a fossil of a brain. But scientists can still find an empty space where the brain used to be.

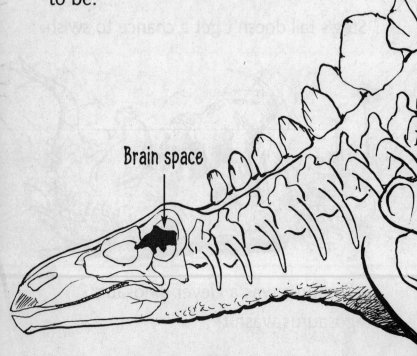

Brain space

Stegosaurus was a big dinosaur. But the space for its brain was tiny!

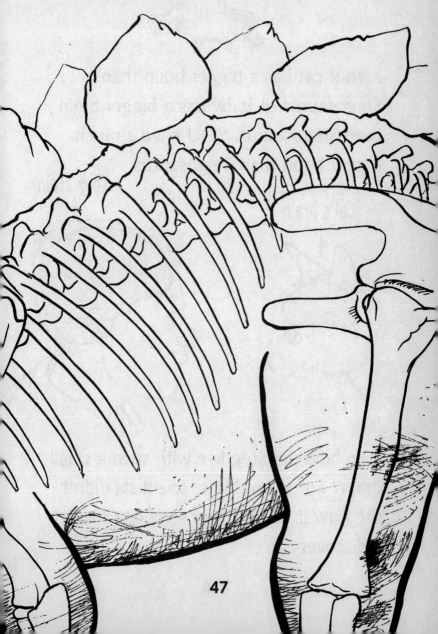

This is how big it *really* was!

Your cat has a bigger brain than Stegosaurus. A baby has a bigger brain than Stegosaurus. YOU have a much bigger brain than Stegosaurus.

Cat's brain

Your brain

So how did Steg live with such a small brain? For a long time, scientists didn't see how it could. Then someone made a discovery.

There was a second space in Steg's skeleton just like the space for its brain. It was much bigger than the first. And nearer to Steg's bottom than its head! They thought Steg had a second brain.

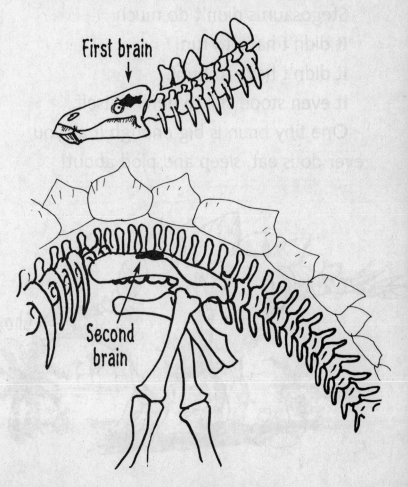

First brain

Second brain

Scientists thought Stegosaurus needed a second brain because it was so big. Now they think that the space near the bottom held nerves that controlled Steg's legs and tail. But it wasn't really a brain.

Stegosaurus didn't do much.

It didn't have to run.

It didn't have to hunt.

It even stood still to defend itself.

One tiny brain is big enough if all you ever do is eat, sleep and plod about!

Chomp!

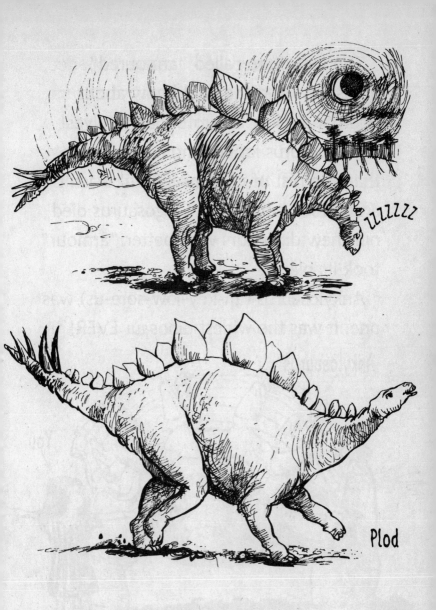

ZZZZZZ

Plod

And besides, Stegosaurus was part of
a group of pea-brained dinosaurs…

The group are called "armoured" dinosaurs. And they did know about one thing. How to protect themselves!

Stegosaurus looked more interesting than the rest of its family. But it wasn't around for long. After Stegosaurus died out, new dinosaurs with better "armour" took its place.

Ankylosaurus (an-key-low-sore-us) was one. It was the widest dinosaur EVER!

Ankylosaurus

You

It had bony plates with sharp spikes all the way from its head to its tail!

Thump!

Its tail ended in a huge, bony club! Ouch!

Euoplocephalus (you-op-low-sef-ah-lus) was a bit smaller. It had loads of armour and a tail-club, too. It was so well protected that it even had bony plates over its eyelids!

If anything tried to attack, Euoplocephalus just tucked its legs in and sat down!

Then nothing could get at its soft belly
and its tiny brain was safe inside that
bony skull!

Like Steg it could swish its tail to
defend itself. But it didn't need to very
often. A dinosaur would have to be
desperate – or daft – ever to think about
attacking Euoplocephalus!

Stegosaurus gets famous

Stegosaurus wasn't the only dinosaur with spiky plates on its spine. There were different stegosaurs in different parts of the world.

Tuojiangosaurus (too-oh-yee-ang-oh-sore-us) came from China. It's got a great big name. But its plates were quite neat and small. And it was only a bit taller than your dad.

Your dad

Tuojiangosaurus

Kentrosaurus (ken-troh-sore-us) came from Africa. The plates on its spine looked much sharper than Steg's. And two long spikes stuck out of its shoulders! It looked nasty, but Kentrosaurus was even smaller than Tuojiangosaurus.

Kentrosaurus

Your dad

But Stegosaurus was the first spiked dinosaur ever discovered. And, it was the biggest of the lot!

A dinosaur expert called
Othniel Charles Marsh
dug up the first
Stegosaurus bones in
Wyoming, North
America, 130 years ago.
One year later he found a complete
skeleton, but the bones had shifted out
of place. It was difficult to see what this
creature was really like.

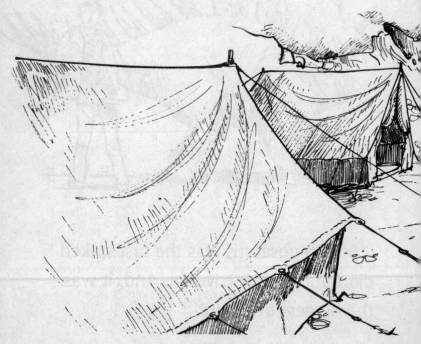

Marsh kept looking for dinosaur bones. He found loads of new types of dinosaur. Then, after ten years, he found a whole Stegosaurus skeleton, with almost all its bones in place. He got a really good idea of what this dinosaur looked like.

Marsh called it Stegosaurus, which means "roof lizard", because he thought its plates looked like roof tiles!

But the plates weren't joined to the body. They didn't connect with any other bones. They were held in place by the flesh on Steg's back.

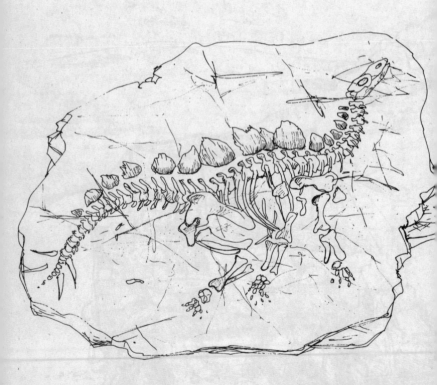

Marsh wasn't sure where the spiky plates fitted on the spine:

Did they lie flat on Steg's back?

Was there one row of plates, or two?

Did they flap up and down?

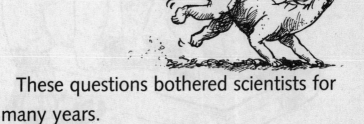

These questions bothered scientists for many years.

Then, just 20 years ago, a skeleton was finally found that had all the plates in place...

At last experts could say for certain that:

The plates stood up on the spine and they didn't flap!

I'm right

But even today, some scientists think the spiky plates stood in one row and others think they stood in two.

In the whole world, only 12 Stegosaurus skeletons have ever been found – and just one baby. So until someone makes a fantastic new discovery, scientists have still got a lot to argue about.

No you're not

**Now you know a lot about
Stegosaurus, which dinosaur
will you discover next?**

T.REX

the DINOSAUR with the stupid smile

IGUANODON

the DINOSAUR with the fat bottom

● Coming soon ●

DIPLODOCUS

the DINOSAUR with the loooong neck

**Now You Know!
The facts you WANT to know**